The Only One in the Room

How I learned to be kinder to myself to be better for others

Marlon M. Woods

THE ONLY ONE IN THE ROOM

HOW I LEARNED TO BE BETTER TO MYSELF TO BE BETTER FOR OTHERS

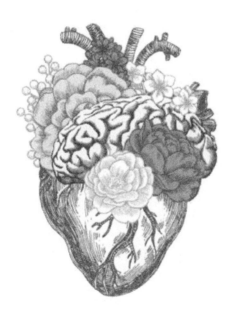

MARLON M. WOODS

This book is dedicated in its entirety to my mother and my grandmother. For showing me what true determination, humility, and sacrifice look like, and for personifying strength in a way no person ever has before.

Acknowledgments

I have been fortunate to live a life full of supportive people. There are many names that do not appear in this book but have so much to do with the person I am today.

To my father, I thank you for choosing me and for my competitive spirit.

To my Uncle Vic and Aunt Sheila, thank you for providing a safe place, a haven, and thank you for showing us love, care, and compassion.

To Ashley, you are the big sister I didn't know I needed. Thank you for keeping us humble, thank you for helping my mother and my sister, and thank you for never letting us win.

To my brothers: Justin, Jon, Black, Zay, Mike, Jamal, Abel, Hayes, Bake, Mahdi, B, Nick, Jessup, Bump, Kizzy, Jason, and Holmes, please know we have all, even if unknowingly, watched and helped each other grow into the men we are today. You were and are my examples of how to be the best I possibly can. It is because of you, I am who I am, and for that I am forever indebted to you.

To you, Coach Danielle Hobson-Lynch, thank you for believing in us. Thank you for demanding more than our best, thank you for holding us accountable, and thank you for being our lighthouse when we were lost at sea.

To my newest best friend, Rebekah, you will never know the true extent of your influence on me, and just how much I look up to and admire you. You have taught and given me more than you know and for that, I am one of the most fortunate people on the planet.

And lastly, to you, holding this book, I give you my thanks, my love, and my admiration. Your support, encouragement, love, passion, enthusiasm, and belief is why you are able to read these very words. Please know there is not a day I do not appreciate you. Please know I will always be a beacon and a light, and please know I will never tire.

I love you all. M.

Prologue

    This book started as a story of my life and evolved into a collection of lessons I have learned through happiness, heartache, triumph, and near defeat. My intention is for you to walk away from this book seeing how I have learned to treat myself better and what my life and experiences have taught me, in the hope that someone, even if it is one person, relates to this and realizes that they are not alone. You can use this book however you like; whether you want to read it all in one go and go back and reference or maybe you want to take it a passage at a time—whatever works for you, works for me. This book is for those who want to look inward to improve themselves and to be better for those who experience life with and around us. Not every passage will resonate with you, and every lesson or learning may not be relevant to you. I hope even if it is only one passage, one sentence, or one quote, it changes you for the better. I hope that when you put this book down, you are in one way or another, a better person because of it.

<u>Regarding the self . . .</u>

"To be yourself in a world that is constantly trying to make you something else is the greatest accomplishment." – Ralph Waldo Emerson

<u>1</u>

If you think about it, one of the easiest things to do should be being yourself. The problem is we have gotten to a point where our social currency is based on what others think of the person we are and not on who we truly are. As we age, we learn to attach a significant portion of our value to the opinions of others. We change what we say, what we wear, and what we think, based on whether it increases or decreases our social currency. Think about this; the likelihood of you existing is approximately 1 in 400 quadrillions. That is the likelihood that your parents were brought into existence, that they met each other, and stayed together long enough to conceive you to create the exact combination of atoms, cells, DNA and alleles that created you, after which you then must survive gestation and alas, birth. And we're not even talking about grandparents yet. Your existence alone is a literal miracle. So, the next time you're doubting yourself or criticizing yourself, remember, the fact that you are here is more than enough. You are 1 in 400 quadrillions.

<u>2</u>

When I was in the first grade, we had Show & Tell the Friday after Christmas break. Ms. Perkins told us to pick our favorite Christmas gift and bring it in for the class to see. I was so excited I could hardly sleep because I knew exactly what gift I was bringing. My mom had gotten me a big laser gun from Toys "R" Us that was black and orange, lit up, making noise, and took six D batteries so it packed a punch. I came to school with a smile a mile wide and could barely contain myself until Show & Tell. After I entered class, I sat down at my desk, smiling, chest out, and head up, toy on the desk—the proudest I had ever been. Well, my moment never came because people were obsessed with the Game Boy another kid had brought to class. Not one person asked about my laser gun and out of sheer embarrassment, after school, I threw my favorite gift away. I allowed what others thought of my gift to change how I felt about it. I allowed my happiness to be dictated by others. We all have people, places, things, and experiences we value in our lives. Treasure them and do your best not to let what others think of them change how special they may be to you.

<u>3</u>

Being unaware of what may be triggering certain behaviors in our lives is dangerous for our mental well-being. Internal and external awareness allows us to understand how we are responding to our environment and how those behaviors are manifesting. Sometimes we find ourselves feeling strong emotions or uncertain why we feel uneasy or not ourselves. Have you ever been in a bad mood or quieter than normal and not sure why? Often, if we take some time to truly be inquisitive concerning ourselves and our emotions, we can unveil underlying stimuli that may be triggering certain feelings. Take time to be with yourself and to understand that our minds may not always be who we are. Our environments—physical, mental, social, and spiritual—have a significant influence on our inner voices. Be sure that when you speak to yourself or when you ask yourself questions about your life and surroundings, you are doing your best to speak to your true self. This is where we can best identify what may be impacting us and why.

<u>4</u>

Do not neglect how connected the mind and body are. Things as simple as sunlight help regulate our mood and serotonin levels which help us with sleep and emotional regulation. You experience the physical world mentally, physically, and emotionally. Taking care of your body can be a simple but effective way to improve your mental health. The mind experiences what the body perceives and vice versa— both are inextricably linked. When the body needs movement or rest, it is the mind that tells us so, when the mind needs movement or rest it is our body that tells us so. Listen to your body and be honest and kind with yourself mentally and physically. Stress manifests mentally and physically, emotions manifest mentally and physically; our mental and physical worlds are the same. So, whether it is a mental or physical obstacle make sure the first place you look to overcome it is inside.

<u>5</u>

Emotions are one of the most mysterious occurrences we come across in our lives. Seemingly intangible things, ethereal almost, can cause us literal physical pain, stress, and turmoil. Terms such as *heartbreak* and the *pit of the stomach* place these abstract concepts in our world and our bodies. When we allow emotions to linger it feels as if no matter what we do we cannot seem to shake them and often we struggle to define exactly how we feel and why. But if we are inquisitive about our emotions, we begin to understand how fleeting and impermanent they are. Ask yourself, what does this emotion feel like? What color is it? What texture? Where is it? Is it a dense, cold, black block in the pit of your stomach? Is it a warm pink cloud in your chest? As we begin to think about what and where these emotions reside in us, they begin to fade away as we remove the uncertainty. Remember, good or bad, emotions come and go. Marcus Aurelius says: "Reflect often on the speed with which all things in being, or coming into being, are carried past and swept away. Existence is like a river in ceaseless flow, its actions a constant succession of change, its causes innumerable in their variety: scarcely anything stands still, even what is most immediate."

<u>6</u>

Marcus Aurelius said: "Universe, your harmony is my harmony: nothing in your good time is too early or too late for me. All is right that happens in the world. Examine this saying carefully, and you will find it true". Society has this way of mandating and imposing certain standards on the individual. There are certain jobs you should have, certain cars you should drive, certain pay, certain social media apps, certain phone brands, shoes, clothes, neighborhoods, cities, tattoos, hair, makeup, facial hair, body shape, relationship status—you name it; there is a standard for it. The issue with this societal "norm" is who defines the norm? Who is the final authority on what we're supposed to do and not supposed to do? Constantly measuring ourselves and our lives against this social yardstick creates a state of constant criticism and dissatisfaction because no matter what you do, you can't seem to catch up. Disregard these standards. Where you are today, who you are today, and what you are today is all you have and all that matters. You may think you are not where you are supposed to be, driving the car you're supposed to drive, in the relationship you're supposed to be in, but rest assured, no matter your circumstances, no matter the time or the place, you are exactly where you need to be.

<u>7</u>

Our lives have been engineered to make us the main character. We only get the emails that are sent to us, receive the calls that are meant for us. We only get notifications about ourselves when we're mentioned, tagged, liked, or highlighted. We always see the world from our point of view. This seems straightforward until we start to think about how this can begin to skew our perception of the world and how we interact with it. I went through a period of experiencing spotlight syndrome. I was under the impression that everyone was always talking about me. I was leading myself to believe that all attention was focused on me—good and bad. This led to an increase in anxiety when dealing with social media, but what manifested as the most dangerous was I began to value myself based on that attention. Thankfully I became aware of this and to this day make sure to remind myself the world does not revolve around me. Every person is the main character in their life, but always remember we're never the only film playing.

<u>8</u>

There was a time when I was trying inexplicably hard to be a lot of things I wasn't. I was under the impression for me to gain the agency of others, the support and approval of others I needed to be what they liked. I felt I needed to do the things other men did, I needed to look the way they looked, dress the way a "man" was supposed to dress, and even post on social media the way men posted—not the dancing and animated characters I wanted to post about. One day I was at work, and I told myself I couldn't post something I wanted to because people would judge me. That became the day I decided to focus on what made me happy rather than focusing on what would make others happy. Many of us are denying what truly makes us happy out of fear of disapproval and judgment from others. I had to learn that regardless of what you do or don't do, people will think what they want. This isn't about not caring what others think, it's about not giving what others think the power to change who you are.

<u>9</u>

In a year, the average person will cross paths with roughly 19,000 people. Consider that 3.5 billion people use social media for an average of 2.5 hours per day and you see just how easy it is for that number to quadruple. We deal with dozens, hundreds, even thousands of images, videos, and in-person interactions with other humans each week. We see perfectly scripted videos, edited and curated images, and convenient snapshots of life from thousands of people. We compare ourselves to the moment, we judge ourselves based on the output, we compare our two weeks to someone else's 20 years, we assume no one would ever make our mistakes. It is important to remember that everyone has their race to run, and we all start that race at different places and different times. Do not ridicule and criticize yourself for not being where you think you're supposed to be simply because someone else is there. It's not always the case that you're behind, or lazy, or an underachiever—you're simply running your race.

10

There's a YouTube channel called Impact Theory, and, in an episode, Tom Bilyeu spoke about the proverbial "overnight celebrity" or the person who "came out of nowhere." We are all familiar with the term, but we may not realize it often; we make others great to let ourselves off the hook. When we assume that someone is an overnight success, we disregard all the hard work they have done to be afforded the opportunities they were given and to be prepared for those opportunities. When we call someone an overnight success, we say to ourselves: "What they have achieved is unattainable and no matter how hard I work that will never be me, so what's the point?" We self-impose these limitations and mental barriers to justify hitting the snooze button or skipping the last set. I am very aware that there are some people who you may deem undeserving of their success or status, but regardless, do your best not to sell yourself short. You are capable of so much more than you know; you just have to be willing to believe you can do it.

11

Have you ever noticed that weeds, no matter the soil, climate, location, or care, always flourish? Weeds do not need attention, weeds do not need time, they require no effort on our part, no special treatment, fertilizer, or nutrients. If you want to grow weeds all you need to do is nothing and they will appear and flourish. Weeds are resilient, and once they have borne their roots, they are difficult to get rid of. But what about flowers? What about roses, daffodils, tiger lilies, or orchids? These require time, energy, attention, care, and effort, but when they flower, their harvest is beautiful, and pleasant, and brings joy to all who see them. Negative thoughts such as jealousy, resentment, contempt, anger, and spite are like weeds. All they need to flourish is for us not to think about what we say and not give attention to our thoughts, words, and actions. When we act in this manner, we produce weeds. It is easy to react to situations, easy to be angry, to judge, to act out of spite. It requires much more effort to take the higher road, to meet hate with compassion, to meet resent with empathy. Treat your mind like a fresh garden. Allow it to its own devices and your garden will be overrun by weeds, but give it the time, effort, and attention it needs, and your garden will produce beautiful flowers.

<u>12</u>

One of the hardest things about changing is admitting that there is something that can be improved. There are numerous reasons why someone may want to change; self-improvement, relationships, work, wellness, spirituality, or ethics—to name a few. Sometimes, the decision to change is of our own volition, and other times it is brought to our attention. When considering decisions about changing, try thinking about constant improvement. When we think about improvement, we take away the negative connotation of our current state. Every step you have ever taken is a step. This step may be forward, it may be backward, but so long as your pursuit is in the direction of a better you than yesterday, you have been successful in said pursuit. Do not make the act of change about destroying who you are because who you are today is the foundation of who you will be tomorrow.

<u>13</u>

The discipline of body image often comprises of those who believe people should look a certain way, those who feel there is an appropriate height, weight, and composition, those that rebuke said standards and many who judge others based solely on the way they look. People struggle with every aspect of the way; be it height, weight, size, face, teeth, skin, even as specific as facial hair. What we often assume is people are what they look like. If you look a certain way, then you must be a certain way. This is simply not the case. And the sooner we teach people to love who they are and accept who they are and what they've been given, the sooner we can move to a place where we understand one of the most important parts of being human is valuing yourself. We all have our demons, and we all have those mornings we wake up and we just don't feel attractive. Look at yourself, see yourself, love yourself, and value yourself. Because regardless of what shortcomings you may think you have, we must learn to love ourselves, truly, before we can begin to appreciate just how special we all are.

<u>14</u>

When I first began meditating the hardest part about mindfulness was being alone with my thoughts. My mind would wander, and I would become acutely aware of decisions I had made, thoughts I had, and words I said. I found myself in a room, alone, lying to myself in my mind. Justifying my actions or inaction, making excuses for my behavior. There are times in your life when you are being overly critical. Times when perhaps you could treat yourself with more grace, allow yourself the rest you need, and time to appreciate what you have accomplished. However, there are also times when you must be honest with yourself. This doesn't mean berate, denigrate, or disparage yourself, rather, ask yourself honest questions and give honest answers. The hardest person to be honest with is yourself because only you know the truth, and when faced with an image of yourself that is not ideal, you resist. A less than ideal image of yourself is more than ok, none of us are perfect. But to be dishonest with yourself is to betray your very being. Treat yourself the way you'd want someone to treat you, with honor, respect, and love. Be comfortable with your thoughts and your being. Being alone is one thing, being by yourself is another. Learn to love that person.

<u>15</u>

When I was in college, I had a football strength coach who was probably one of the most passionate and intense individuals I have ever met. Coach Field was a retired Marine and had biceps that could fill any sleeve they entered. One weekend we lost to Colgate, and they scored 52 points on us. The next time we had training he made us carry 25 lbs. over our heads for 52 rounds of stairs in the stadium and then made us curl 65 lbs. for 52 reps on his count. Hands down one of the most gut-wrenching workouts I have ever done. As he tormented us, he asked why he was the angriest person in the room? Why didn't that loss upset us as much as it did him? He said it was because we didn't take it personally. Sure it's "just a game" but at the end of the day, we were outworked, outplayed, and outhustled. He took that loss personally as a strength. To him, it was a direct reflection of him as a coach and he felt it should have reflected our effort and skill. He was right. Is life always about winning? Depends on who you ask, but often in life we take losses on the chin, we don't learn from our losses, or we allow others to walk over us. This isn't about vengeance or always needing to win, it's about self-worth. The next time you "lose" ask yourself, what can you do to be better next time? The next time you're disrespected or disregarded ask yourself what you can learn from that experience? Take it personally. Let it fuel your next victory.

<u>16</u>

At times it may seem as if life is happening to us. It may feel like we have no say, it may feel like we are helpless; we feel like we don't have a choice. Regardless of the situation, circumstances, or influences, there is always a choice to be made. Each thought, word, or action, whether it comes to fruition or not is a choice. We decided whether to wear that outfit, we decided whether to text our loved one, we decided if we want to answer the call. No matter the choice you make or do not make, a choice has always been made. Remember this and have an honest inward look as you reflect on choices you have or haven't made in your life.

<u>17</u>

All of us understand the concept of living like there is no tomorrow. We understand what people mean when they say live each day like it's your last, and we all remember when *carpe diem* took the world by storm. However, this isn't about a bucket list, or buying the car you've always wanted, or even making sure that if today were the last you'd have no regrets. We all have things we wish we could have done better; we all have a bucket list somewhere, we all have "what if" conversations, but what we don't consider is the limits we unconsciously put on ourselves. When we think about the what-ifs and the worst-case scenarios one of the first things we do is remove all burdens, limitations, and boundaries, and then we talk about all the things we would love to do. What if we applied that approach to our lives as they are now? How much more could we achieve? How much happier would we be? This doesn't mean to disregard all your responsibilities or eat, pray, and love yourself into a cave in Tibet. It's meant to remind us not to pace ourselves too much. As we consciously or unconsciously hold ourselves back day-to-day we may be reinforcing the idea of what we can't do. I say live life full speed. Rest can come later.

One of the hardest times of my life was when I was struggling financially during the time we had opened our gym in Augusta, GA. The rent, electricity, water, phone bill, food, gas, and my dog were the only things I could barely afford to maintain month after month. Decisions between toilet paper and paper towels were some of the hardest decisions I have ever made but not because I needed both, rather because I never thought I would need to choose. One of the hardest feelings to overcome during this time was the feeling of hunger. What was interesting about my experience is that it was less about the pain and discomfort of hunger and more about the uncertainty of when relief would come. Will the next meal be enough? Will I have to go to sleep hungry again? Tupac said: "For every dark night, there's a brighter day." Those moments when we are isolated, when the silence is so loud it's deafening, when the darkness is suffocating, and when the stress is nauseating, that is when we need that message—but it is also when we are least likely to hear it. So, if you happen to come across this passage at a time when you feel like you won't make it; whether it's pain, trauma, or uncertainty; if you feel like you're drowning, find comfort in knowing that all things, good and bad, come to an end. We cannot have highs without lows and cannot have light without darkness. The dichotomy of life is the beauty of life. You just make it one more day. Just one.

19

We often fall victim to the trap of trying to compare our day one to someone else's day 100. One of the hardest fears to overcome is the fear of starting; the worry that it will be hard, the fear that you'll never be good enough. Procrastination is apprehension; it's an expectation of fear, a worry of difficulty. We underestimate the power of consistency and the role it plays in improvement. Do not get caught up in comparison. Don't worry about it sucking or not being as good in the beginning because it's never good at the beginning for anyone. Nothing is insurmountable and you'll never know how much you're capable of until you start. You never have to be great to start, but you do have to start to be great. Give yourself some time, your day one does not define you.

<u>20</u>

For the first 27 years of my life, I was adamant about making others happy. I wanted to be the funniest, I wanted to be liked, I wanted to be admired, I wanted to be needed. Almost everything I did was in some shape or form because I wanted to make sure someone else was happy. What this inevitably led to was an inability to express myself, and a further inability of those in my life to comprehend my actions and words once I attempted to express my emotions and desires. Ironically, it wasn't until my first marriage ended that I was forced to face not always being the good guy. Dealing with conflict, expressing myself honestly and openly, and not doing something because it was best for someone else. This was my first lesson in understanding the difference between pleasing others and serving others, and I am still learning each day.

<u>21</u>

One of my favorite movies is *The Pursuit of Happyness*, for more reasons than I can list. One of my favorite scenes is when Chris Gardner, played by Will Smith, says, "Don't ever let someone tell you, you can't do something. Not even me. You got a dream, you got to protect it. People can't do something themselves; they want to tell you you can't do it. You want something, go get it. Period." Whenever someone in your life trusts you enough to share their dreams and aspirations with you, the worst thing you can do is be anything less than supportive. A person's dreams are sacred, personal, and intimate. Your dreams are often where some of your strongest sentiments and desires are housed, so you should protect them, cherish them, and never be ashamed or afraid to pursue them. No matter how outlandish, or how ridiculous you may think your desires are, everything that has ever been done started as just a dream.

We have all heard the words "I don't care what other people think." What this phrase creates is more of avoidance or ignorance to the fact that other people have opinions and shields us from the fact that judgment exists. It's hard to post a picture and not receive the likes or comments you want to. It's hard when people do not agree with your point of view, and I'm certain we have all experienced the physical sickness that comes with a rejection of any kind—be it personal or professional. Disagreements, opinions, judgment, rejection; they're all a part of life and we all experience them but it's when we begin to put our worth solely in the opinions of others that we begin to tread into the murky water. Of course, we do care what others think at times, but it should not solely determine our actions or opinions. Another one of my favorite Marcus Aurelius quotes is: "Everything in any way beautiful has its beauty of itself, inherent and self-sufficient: praise is no part of it. At any rate, praise does not make anything better or worse . . ." Remember this next time you question your worth.

Marlon M. Woods

<u>23</u>

Malcolm X said, "You can't separate peace from freedom because no one can be at peace unless he has his freedom." Malcolm X may have been speaking about a different type of freedom when he said this in 1965, but when I hear this, I think about how much pressure we put on ourselves day in and day out. When we learn to "free" ourselves of the comparison, self-hate, critiques, and judgment of ourselves we give ourselves peace; the calm that comes with comfort with ourselves, the confidence that comes with the composure we have with our most basic self. No titles, no salary, no address, no car, no status . . . just us. When we can come to terms with the person we are and can look that person in the mirror stripped of all our qualifiers and without any judgment, that's when we have truly been freed; that is when we have truly found peace.

<u>24</u>

When I first started teaching Les Mills, I would film myself in the mirror for hours. Comments like: it's not that serious, wow, that's a bit much, you must enjoy that, relax, and my favorite, you have too much time on your hands, were frequent occurrences. These comments make you second-guess yourself, make you feel insecure and uncertain about what you are pursuing. CT Fletcher said: "Greatness cannot be achieved without obsession." I believe greatness requires obsession. The average person cannot relate to an extreme passion, to an obsession, so when they come across someone deeply passionate and driven the natural response is to attack that person by projecting their insecurities and displacing their frustration. Chase your dreams, work hard, and whatever you do, do not allow yourself to be deterred by those in the stands. Because if you fail, "at least you fail while daring greatly, so that your place shall never be with those cold and timid souls who neither know victory nor defeat." – Theodore Roosevelt

<u>25</u>

I have known four people who have taken their own lives. Suicide is something that happens every single day and no matter how many resources we have, no matter how much awareness we raise, the bottom line is, when someone is at the point that they are contemplating suicide, they go out of their way to isolate themselves and even the strongest message, the most compassionate friend, will have trouble reaching them. No matter how bright the light, the darkness that surrounds suicide is suffocating and unforgiving. I have had my struggles with suicide, brought on by immense financial pressure and exacerbated by the vicious cycle of depression. What helped me the most was my mother and the thought of what my suicide would do to her. I watched a Sherlock Holmes series once and he said, "Taking your own life. Interesting expression. Taking it from who? Once it's over, it's not you who'll miss it. Your own death is something that happens to everybody else. Your life is not your own. Keep your hands off it." I am not here to tell anyone what to do or not to do while in the throes of depression and battling with suicide, but what I do know is no matter how dark and how alone you feel, you are never alone. It feels impossible to overcome, it feels endless and relentless; but if you can remember that you have made it through 100% of your bad days and each day you wake up is another victory—step by step you will make your way back to the light.

<u>26</u>

One of the most inspirational people in my life is my stepbrother, Dez. Dez is a few years older than me and doesn't have the cleanest track record in the world, but when I met Dez he was well on his way to working as hard as he could to provide for his children and completely change his life. I watched Dez work 12–16-hour days sometimes and not once did he ever complain. Not once did he ever regret anything he had done; not once did he ever shift blame. Each day he worked he held his head high, whether it was going to work at the factory, Burger King, or the hospital. To this day he has no idea just how much he inspires me and what he taught me. In the movie *The Equalizer*, in response to someone saying, "Not in my world," Denzel Washington responds with "Then change your world." Dez taught me sometimes you must do something you may not want to do to change your world, and even though it may not be comfortable, it may be required. Thank you, bro.

<u>27</u>

In my first year of college, I all but failed every class. I know we don't all use the same grading scales, but a 0.80 GPA is about as low as they get. I was at risk of being kicked out of school and sent back home, forfeiting football and track in the process. I was placed on academic probation and was faced with a choice, either throw in the towel or begin the long and difficult trek to pull my GPA back up to a respectable number. There is nothing more daunting than fighting for something when you know the odds are against you, but often there is no time that fighting is more important. I had to attend school year-round for the next three years, but I proved to myself that I was willing to fight even though the odds were against me. It's easy to fight when you're supposed to win, it's easy to remain calm, composed, and confident when you have the lead, but it's those times when you must overcome the ultimate that show us how much we're capable of. Never shy away from a fight for something or someone you feel is worth it, because even if you don't win, sometimes just standing back up is a victory in and of itself.

Two of the scariest days of my life were the day I did stand-up comedy for the first time and the day of my first triathlon. I've always been a funny person but being tasked with standing in front of a group of strangers and making them laugh was something I was not ready for. The night before my triathlon the race was at risk of being canceled due to torrential rains but went ahead the next morning, rain and all. I have never been a swimmer and taught myself to swim over the six months before the race. On the day of the comedy show, I couldn't concentrate, couldn't eat, and could barely walk because of nerves. The morning of my triathlon I was shaking so much I spilled blueberries all over the kitchen floor. I had never been more paralyzed by fear than I was on these two days in the same year. At the beginning of 2020, I made a promise to myself to make myself uncomfortable, to challenge myself. These experiences, though traumatic, are important to experience in life. We've all heard the saying that growth happens outside of the comfort zone, but it is so much easier said than done. The choice is yours: "one day" or "day one."

<u>29</u>

When it comes to self-awareness there are two aspects, internal and external. Internal self-awareness is your understanding of yourself, your values, your ethics, what drives and motivates you. External awareness is knowing how others perceive you, how they view you. This is not the same as being what others want you to be; this is making sure we are aware of how our thoughts, words, and actions are manifesting externally. For example, when I first moved to Australia my wife would sometimes travel for work and I would be desperate for her to return. I understood that I was lonely without her and that I found it difficult to relax when she wasn't around because it was a new country and a new home. What I wasn't aware of was the fact these feelings were manifesting negatively. She said that every time she came home, I was withdrawn, antisocial, and angry as if I was punishing her for leaving. This external self-awareness helped me pinpoint what exactly I was feeling and why I was feeling that way; it allowed me to correct the behavior by communicating how I felt. Many of us go through our lives without having internal or external self-awareness, or sometimes both. It's difficult to look ourselves in the mirror, difficult to be honest with ourselves sometimes, but having that conversation with ourselves can help identify the cause of behaviors we may or may not be aware of.

One of my favorite parts of working on myself—be it exercise and training, school, playing the piano, or writing this book—is the fact that 95% of the work and effort I put into bettering myself is done for me, by me, and without anyone watching. We underestimate how difficult it is for those outliers to put in 10,000 hours of diligent and focused practice into their work. Damian Lillard, an NBA player for the Portland Trail Blazers tweeted one of the most profound sentences I have read recently. He said, "If you want to look good in front of thousands, you have to outwork thousands in front of nobody" and truer words have never been spoken. We see people set out on journeys, we see the start, we see the finish, we may get an update here or there—but most of the work is done without us knowing, without recognition, without praise. No one dreams about practicing piano for thousands of hours, or reading hundreds and hundreds of case files, or playing hundreds of games of tennis. So next time you set your sights on something, be sure to first ask yourself, *what am I willing to accept to get where I need to be?* Results do not come without effort. What we get in life is sometimes determined by how much we are willing to put in. If there's something you've set your eyes on or something you're considering doing, make sure you're doing it for yourself. Make sure you want it bad enough to get through it on the days you don't feel like it, make sure you're not in it for the praise or just for the result. If your "why" is not deeply embedded in you, is not crystal clear, you are leaving the door to quitting open. It's the things we truly want that we work hardest for. Make sure you know what's in your sights and be willing to work towards it even on the days you don't want to because those days matter most.

<u>31</u>

One summer I worked at UPS (United Parcel Service) as an evening loader. UPS ships approximately 21 million packages daily and my job was to stand at the bottom of a conveyor belt at the back of a truck trailer and scan and load each package onto the truck from 4 pm to 9 pm five days a week. One evening I had loaded a trailer faster and neater than I had ever done before, the last box fitting perfectly within a tapestry of boxes to the very end of the truck. It was the first trailer I had finished on my own and I remember looking at it proudly and taking my gloves off for a break. After the hatch closed and the truck pulled off, I was startled by the sound of the hatch opening and a brand new, empty trailer appearing. The buzzer signaling to the sorters that the chute was clear buzzed, and a new stream of boxes began sliding towards me. The defeat I felt was overwhelming, the helplessness paralyzing. With my head hanging, and my shoulders slumped, a veteran in the warehouse walked past me and said, "The boxes never stop, man. The boxes never stop." I took that to heart and reminded myself that each day the sun will rise, clocks will never stop, people will come, people will go, you will hurt, and you will heal. There will be days when you have an empty trailer, there will be days when the sailing is smooth, and there will be days when you feel like you can't breathe. No matter how much life seems to pile on you, if you remember to keep your head up and keep going—even if things get backed up—eventually they will clear.

<u>32</u>

Mike Tyson said, "There is nothing more powerful than a person whose time has come." We forget the most powerful thing on Earth is the human mind. All innovation, all dreams, technology, the greatest feats imaginable have been because of another person just like you believed they could. We underestimate how incredibly unique we are, how—no matter how far away or unachievable something may seem—a human just like you achieved it. I realize there are factors out of our control, genetics, location, age, finances, etc., but don't sell yourself short. The grace and compassion you give others should be the same you give yourself because all of us have what it takes to be everything we want to be; we just must believe that our time has come. Don't forget that you were born to live life to its fullest and that no matter who we are, our time will come to an end. But while you're here, give yourself time to come into your own because you bring what no other person who has ever or will ever be able to bring. Being you is hard but you're the only one who can do it.

33

Every person who dies has lived a full life. We have all lost loved ones before their time, but you cannot lose what you do not have. Always live your life grateful for the gift of living. I do my best to honor the privilege of life each day. I work on being as present and as grateful for my life in its entirety each day—my breath, my heart, my eyes, my hands, my legs, my home, my family, my friends–all of it. I will not say much but will leave you with this quote from Marcus Aurelius: "At break of day, when you are reluctant to get up, have this thought ready to mind: 'I am getting up for a man's work. Do I still then resent it, if I am going out to do what I was born for, the purpose for which I was brought into the world? Or was I created to wrap myself in blankets and keep warm?' 'But this is more pleasant.' Were you then born for pleasure - all for feeling, not for action? Can you not see plants, birds, ants, spiders, bees all doing their own work, each helping in their own way to order the world? And then you do not want to do the work of a human being - you do not hurry to the demands of your own nature. 'But one needs rest too.' One does indeed: I agree. But nature has set limits to this too, just as it has to eating and drinking, and yet you go beyond these limits, beyond what you need. Not in your actions, though, not any longer: here you stay below your capability." You are beyond amazing, you are beyond excellent, you are beyond beautiful, but often the last person to believe this truth is ourselves. Learn how to treat yourself as you would treat others, for this is the first and most critical lesson in becoming a better person—but often it is the last lesson a person learns thoroughly.

<u>34</u>

One day I found myself in the parking lot of the unemployment office. Unemployment is a very real and common thing in society and any person collecting unemployment is by no means a failure. However, for me, I had felt like I disappointed myself, my mother, and those who believed I would be something better. I hung my head low as I walked into the office, I sat quietly, my head down, my eyes fixed on the ground in front of me. I will never forget the woman who helped me that day, Mrs. Washington. She stood 5 foot 3, curly gray hair, glasses, blue slacks, white blouse, pearl earrings, and a voice that reverberated with the strength of a woman who had decades of life experience. When I went back to her office, she asked me about my circumstances and when I spoke, I avoided eye contact and was barely audible. Mrs. Washington said, "Marlon, lift your head" and when I did, I saw a sign she had showing directly behind her head pinned to the wall of her cubicle. It was Proverbs 4: 25-27: "Keep your head up, your eyes straight ahead, and your focus fixed on what is in front of you. Take care you don't stray from the straight path, the way of truth, and you will safely reach the end of your road." Crazy how the universe works sometimes. No matter how low you may feel, you have absolutely nothing to be ashamed of. If you want to get where you're going, you must keep your eyes focusing forward. Lift your head and keep it there, because I've been in that same seat before, and that seat does not define you. You define you.

Marlon M. Woods

The Only One in the Room

<u>Regarding others . . .</u>

"Love and kindness are never wasted. They always make a
difference. They bless the one who receives them, and they bless you,
the giver."
– Barbara de Angelis

<u>1</u>

One time, an Uber Eats order took longer than expected and once the order arrived, the rider went up and down my street looking for the address which took an extra five minutes. Frustrated because I was hungry, irritated, and because this stranger did not know exactly where I lived, when the food arrived, I ripped the door of the building open and stormed down the front steps only to be met by an extremely apologetic and worried rider. I had a moment of extreme external awareness and saw this image of myself angry, ungrateful, and excessively entitled. I am beyond grateful that I was able to experience this with some awareness of what was going on. Be kind to others and go out of your way to be understanding. Do your best never to assume anyone knows how bad your day has been, how hungry you are, or that your apartment is up the elevator on the left . . . and most of all never yell at your Uber driver.

<u>2</u>

I've been fortunate to have people in my life who believed in me and been willing to do so even in the face of adversity or contest. My track coach saw in me what I refused to see in myself. One of my best friends, Abel, was willing to give me a chance when others refused to do so. Without the advocacy of Jacquelynne and KG, I am not sure I would even be in the position to write these very words. Having people who have believed in me has reminded me how important it is to advocate for others. Loyalty comes in many forms, belief in others comes in many forms, and trust comes in many forms. This is a reminder to advocate for others when you can, to believe in others when they are unsure of themselves. We have no idea how unsure some people feel, and we underestimate how much of an impact we can have if someone knows you believe in them.

<u>3</u>

We live in a world of friends and followers. Hundreds, thousands, and millions of people are labeled friends. The overuse of the word has desensitized what it means to be close to someone. In a time of oversharing and under-connecting, of over-exposure and hyper-judgment, we forget how much value should be placed on those you have built a genuine and safe connection with. I made the mistake of lying to someone very important to me, and it destroyed me. It made me feel cheap and it made me feel insecure to the point I couldn't bring myself to speak about it nor address the situation. My friend and I did not talk for months and when we finally did, the weight had been lifted off my chest, but not completely until I formally addressed my wrongdoing and apologized. I was reminded how important and how sacred a true friendship is in a time when everyone is a "friend." If you are fortunate enough to have people in your life who you can confide in, who you trust, who you love, who show no judgment or agenda, be sure you always honor those people. Though we live in the most connected era of human existence it has become harder and harder to stay connected.

<u>4</u>

We've heard the saying "You are the sum of the five people you spend the most time with" and we are familiar with the saying that you attract what you want and if you have in your mind something you want, your desire plays an integral part in ensuring you receive it. Michael Bernard Beckwith said, "You don't attract what you want, you attract what you are." He was speaking about the frequency we vibrate on, and this made me think about the people we associate with. At certain points in my life, I have found myself surrounded by very negative people, very small-minded people, very judgmental people, very cynical people. And when I look back at these periods of my life, I realize it was because I was being those very things. What I was doing, the decisions I was making, my thoughts and my actions were attracting those types of people. When I changed the frequency I was vibrating on it changed what and who I attracted to myself. This works both ways because people who are not vibrating on the same frequency as you will not feel comfortable around you and slowly but surely you will part ways. If you are finding yourself surrounded by people or things that are making you feel off or unlike yourself, check your frequency and check those around you as well. When you find people you resonate with, treat those around you as though they are a part of you, allow your waves to sync, and see how much you grow together.

<u>5</u>

In a book I read about Buddhism, there's an analogy that likened an angry person to a bull in the field. If there is an angry bull thrashing about in a field you wouldn't immediately go to subdue the bull, doing your best to match his energy and aggression, because then both of you will end up exhausted—and more than likely one or both of you are going to be injured. Rather than attacking the bull head-on, a better approach may be to allow the bull to tire itself out and then go calmly to subdue the bull. When we encounter someone angry or frustrated or someone we disagree with, we often try to go blow for blow; meeting their aggression with ours. When this happens, you end up saying things you don't mean and walking away feeling worse than before. What if we approached others the same way we approached the bull, by mincing our words and using discernment, precision, and gentleness when speaking to others? If someone is angry with us or insults us, or is abusive or manipulative, what if we asked ourselves what they are going through and why they may be acting that way rather than just reacting to what that person has said or done? Bringing compassion to conflict is like bringing an ambulance to an accident rather than more chaos. Dr. Martin Luther King Jr. said, "Darkness cannot drive out darkness; only light can do that. Hate cannot drive out hate; only love can do that."

<u>6</u>

One day I was teaching one of my group fitness classes and a woman came into class and settled in the back row, close to the door. I taught the class just as I would any other and carried on with my evening, again, not thinking twice about the class. About a year later, this same woman had never missed a class since. I watched her gain confidence and comfort in the room and eventually became such a staple presence in the class. She came up to me one day and said the first day she came into class was a week after her husband had killed himself. She said she had planned on killing herself later that week. She had already taken off of work and decided on how she would commit the act. She went on to say at one point in the class she and I made eye contact and I said, "Trust me, you absolutely can do this." When she heard those words, she realized she had no business thinking of ending her own life. Had she not come back to class I would have never thought anything of it, but someone would have lost a daughter, a sister, a friend, and their lives would have been forever changed. This is not about what I said or what I did, because I did what I would have done regardless. The point is you never know who is going to come into your classroom, you never know how much eye contact can help someone—an acknowledgment, a compliment, or even just a smile can help someone or change their day. We never really know what someone is going through or what they've been through, so we should always do our best to treat each other with care and compassion because everyone has their own unique story.

<u>7</u>

I read a comment on social media one time and all it said was: "Can you please notice me?" I wasn't prepared for how much this comment would affect me. I was dumbfounded by the simplicity of the comment mixed with the desperation of the tone. I spent time thinking about just how alone some people may feel, how invisible some may feel. I know that I went through a period when I would willingly go days without speaking to anyone; now imagine those that go days without speaking to anyone unwillingly. Unasked for loneliness can lead to depression, anxiety, substance abuse, and even suicide, and many of us go through our lives unaware of the fact that there are people who feel unwanted, unloved, and unseen. Do your best to notice and acknowledge as many people in your life as you can. Whether it's the person walking their dog, the person eating lunch alone, the taxi driver, the CFO, or the gardener—we are all worthy and we are all we have in this world.

<u>8</u>

Social media provides us all with the unique and sometimes dangerous opportunity to interact with people we otherwise would never come across in our lives. This is incredible for forming connections and building networks, learning about different cultures, and diversity of thought. You are also met with more opportunities to disagree, to engage in conflict, and to be exposed to negativity, judgment, and opinions you may otherwise never stumble across. We've all either intentionally or unintentionally been in an online argument and we find ourselves shaking, aggravated, nervous, stressed, anxious, angry, upset—or all the above. Often, the person you are arguing with is nameless and faceless. You have never nor will ever meet this person, yet we invest time, energy, physical, mental, and spiritual well-being into this conflict and at the end of the day, nothing comes of it other than a feeling of distress. Often, the opinion of this faceless communicator will not be changed, neither of you will back down, and you'll walk away wishing you had never engaged; understanding some behaviors and opinions need to be called out or confronted at times. When you find yourself in one of these situations or feel that tension may be escalating, find peace in knowing people will think what they wish, and it is not your job to influence standpoints. Use discernment, patience, discipline, compassion, and any other tools you feel are required to protect your peace and your psychological safety.

<u>9</u>

Do not underestimate the power of unhappiness. One of my favorite sayings is: "Happy people aren't hostile." Visualize a time when you thought, said, or did something rude, spiteful, or mean to someone else. This could be a rude comment or snide remark, could be cutting someone off in traffic, commenting something mean on a social media post, laughing at someone, gossiping about someone, or any number of things. No matter how big or small, think about why you did that and what state of mind you were in. Now think of a time when you were blissfully happy and content. Think of where you were, who you were with, what you were doing. Imagine you're driving to your favorite place to eat or favorite place to watch the sunset, with your favorite person, or on your own. Regardless of the place or people, it's perfect and you're happy. Now think about someone being rude to you, or making a remark, cutting you off in traffic, or not holding a door, or cutting in line. These actions would not affect you anywhere near as much. Often, when we're happy we don't allow ourselves to be impacted by microaggressions or rude remarks. When someone says or does something hostile, no matter how big or small it often comes from a lack of something in their lives. It could be temporary, could be suppressed trauma, could be circumstantial—as small as being upset about something that happened at work and taking that out on a Facebook comment thread. What I am saying is the next time you are met with hostility, think about what is causing it. Extend empathy to this person and realize that for them to behave in that manner something must be creating hostility in their lives. If we approach hostile situations with this mindset and understanding, we much better equip ourselves and others to defuse the situation.

<u>10</u>

One of my favorite books is *How to Win Friends and Influence People* by Dale Carnegie. A quote that has stayed with me since I read this book is: "A person's name is to him or her the sweetest and most important sound in any language." Regardless of the language you speak, someone's name is still the same. To me, this quote isn't about remembering every name of every person you meet as if it is a task or an objective. Rather, it reminds me that each person you come across is a sentient human being, worth just as much as you are. Each person you have ever come across was named by someone, is loved by someone, is missed by someone, and is needed for this world. To me, this is a reminder to all of us never to discard or disregard another human being, and if you are fortunate enough to learn their name, rather than trying to memorize the name, take pleasure in getting to know the human behind the name.

11

Author Agatha Christie said, "Very few of us are what we seem." Truer words have never been spoken. When we come across others it is common and somewhat instinctual for us to make certain assumptions about them. The way they dress, the way they look, walk, smell, what they are doing, their age, if they're married or not, what they drive, dozens of things—all from what sometimes is a mere glance as you pass by someone. It's human nature for us to apply heuristics to interactions with others to ease the cognitive load required daily but taking these shortcuts sacrifices understanding, empathy, and compassion for others. It's quite easy for us to look at others through the lens of our own experiences and understanding of the world but this leads to misinterpretation and misunderstanding. To judge someone is to assume you understand their story, which often, we do not. The next time you come across someone and you find yourself passing judgment try applying curiosity to the situation instead, and not just to them, but yourself also. Why am I passing judgment? Why am I making these assumptions? Where are these feelings or assumptions coming from? How can I change the way I am approaching this situation? How can I better understand this situation or person? If we apply curiosity to this aspect of our nature, we allow ourselves to be more open to others and their experiences and understanding of the world—which will only make us all serving each other better.

<u>12</u>

I used to make it a point to try and argue my way into being proven correct or into a concession of the correctness if there was an argument. Whether it was a girlfriend, a friend, or a stranger, I used to do my best to make sure I was heard. The problem with this way of thinking is that for me to be right, someone else has to be wrong. This may be suitable in a factual debate but where this gets dangerous is when we apply it to loved ones. When we disagree, we sometimes get defensive. This may be pride, anger, fear, or uncertainty we are dealing with, but it leads to the same outcome; one or both parties feeling dejected, upset, closed off, and uncomfortable. Marcus Aurelius said: "Seek the truth because it has never caused harm to anyone, but what has caused harm is to persist in one's own self-deception and ignorance." I like to replace ignorance with arrogance in these circumstances to remind me that even though I may be correct, to make someone else feel wrong doesn't help either person. What I recommend is rather than trying to find rightness, try and find a way for everyone to be heard and seen because being "right" is a short-term outlook. "Seek first to understand, then to be understood." – Stephen Covey

13

I had this good friend a few years ago. We had tons in common, we laughed at work, laughed at the gym; gut-wrenching, stomach pain laughs. It felt like the budding of a lifelong friendship. And then one day it all stopped. I reached out and got no response. For days, then weeks, and then months. One day, finally, after pleading for a response I wish I had never gotten he simply said he was going through a period of growth right now and I just wasn't a part of that. He went on to apologize for not being responsive and that was it. It took me a while to process what had happened and why. I had never "lost" a friend that way before, but the biggest pain point was my ego. I felt embarrassed and offended as if he was directly insulting me and my character. As I gave the situation more time to process and myself time to mature emotionally, I gained admiration and respect for what he showed me; how to set boundaries. A lot of us have friends or acquaintances who are not good for us, they may enable us, they may influence us negatively, and sometimes they may outright envy us and betray us. Yet we remain out of a self-imposed or imaginary obligation to do so because it isn't socially acceptable to leave. Sometimes what's holding you back is in your blind spot, sometimes what's causing you discomfort or pain is so close you can't see it. Do not be afraid to say no, do not be afraid to put yourself first out of fear of missing out or being judged because to grow you need space. And when you're creating space the first things to move are always those within arm's reach.

<u>14</u>

A few years ago, I was in a relationship I felt was taking more than it was giving. Often, things that made me happy made the other person upset or defensive, and when positive things would happen to me, things I assumed we would celebrate, it often ended up in a fight instead. I would make sure to go out of my way to make her feel comfortable and secure, but it seemed the more I achieved, the more resent build up. You may find yourself in a relationship, intimate or platonic, where good news, promotions, opportunities, seeing your friends, traveling, or anything that does not involve the other leads to arguments rather than celebration. When you become aware of the situation it is easy to become defensive and to judge the other person or to assume they are simply jealous. Resist this way of thinking because it only adds to the dissonance and tension within the relationship. This may stem from one person being the source of happiness for the other; perhaps one person is not fulfilled on their own and you have subsidized their happiness. We often use the cup analogy for this—a healthy relationship being two full cups, rather than one constantly pouring into the other. Up to a certain point you may have had enough to give without significantly infringing upon your own happiness; however, when it gets to a point where you feel you have nothing left to give it becomes unsustainable. Make sure you show up to all relationships as a full cup. To be in a relationship with someone else you must first learn how to be in a relationship with yourself because if you or the person you are with is not happy alone, a relationship will only make this more apparent.

<u>15</u>

Until recently I have always viewed my sister as my total opposite. We grew up in the same household but have experienced drastically different outcomes throughout our lives. My sister was quite rebellious when she was young; she was very hostile, disruptive, angry, and apathetic. I assumed this to be due to her failure to achieve what I had as a young child, I assumed that her behavior was her expressing frustration because she did not quite measure up to her stellar older brother—the gleaming embodiment of perfection. Due to this train of thought, my relationship with my sister was anything but amicable to the point we could hardly be around each other for more than five minutes before we argued. One day a few years ago I received a message from my sister that said, "I need your help. I see you inspiring so many people, helping so many people, but you hardly ever talk to me. I just want my big brother back." I cannot articulate the pain I felt after reading this, but I can tell you that at that moment, our entire lives together flashed before my eyes and I realized that my sister wasn't hostile, my sister wasn't angry, my sister wasn't belligerent, attention-seeking, or promiscuous. My sister was in pain. The events of our lives, the tragedy, the heartbreak, our parents' divorce, financial stress, and the added omnipresent pressure of not being just like her older brother backed my sister into a corner. She had been screaming for help our entire lives and I ignored her. With more maturity, more patience, more understanding, less arrogance, and more empathy I was able to see the error of my ways. Marcus Aurelius said: "Accustom yourself not to be disregarding of what someone else has to say: as far as possible enter the mind of the speaker." We cannot possibly know everything people are going through or how something will impact them, but we can always control how we respond to them and the special effort we are putting in to understand.

16

The first mistake I made when I moved to Australia was underestimating the trauma moving countries creates. Though I was moving to live with my now wife, I assumed I would land on my feet. What was unexpected was how hard it would be acclimating to a new country, a new culture, and being stripped of the way of life I had grown accustomed to. When I was in the U.S. I had clout and authority. I had jobs, I had lots of money, I owned a business, I traveled, I had a network, influence, and never a shortage of things to do and people to see. My first week in Australia was the complete opposite. I had no job, all my friends were on the other side of the world, I had nowhere to be, I had hardly anything I could call my own. I truly struggled for my first few months in Australia and on more than one occasion thought I had made the wrong decision. What helped me the most was my wife, Felicity, going out of her way to remind me daily that my money, jobs, titles, gym, network, belongings were not what defined me, were not why she loved me. She made sure I understood who I am is why she loves me. I hadn't realized until I moved to Australia that my entire life I had defined myself by what I could do and what I possessed. I put worth in what I could provide and when she told me it was me she valued I refused to believe her. It is easy to get engrossed in how much money we have, how often we travel, where we work, and what we drive—but none of this makes us who we are. Who we are is who looks at us in the mirror at the beginning and end of every day. No titles, no money, no networks, no net worth—just you. My wife taught me to love myself for who I am, and for that, I am forever grateful. Make sure you value people not for what they can do for you or what they bring to the table; make sure you value them for who they are, because being loved for who you are, not what you are, is one of our basic human needs. Thank you, my rare and Radiant Queen, for being there for me when I was unable to be there for myself.

<u>17</u>

I remember very starkly one day when I was working in Washington, D.C. this woman who was working on a construction crew getting berated by a man going to work who was upset about the traffic the construction was causing. This had nothing to do with her and everything to do with the torment that man was dealing with in his life. I witnessed this abuse and saw the angst it caused the woman and the man she was working with. I carried on with my day but for some reason felt uneasy for the next few days. I found myself wishing I could go back to that moment and speak up, not because the construction workers needed or wanted me to, but because it was the right thing to do. This feeling of regret was small compared to what others may feel, but it strikes a similar chord. Harriet Beecher Stowe said: "The bitterest tears shed over graves are for words left unsaid and deeds left undone." How many times in life have you allowed an opportunity to pass by? How many times could your life have changed for the good without knowing? How many times have you wanted to say something to someone but didn't? One of the biggest mistakes we make as humans is the assumption that there will always be time, that it will be there tomorrow, that we can put things off. Sometimes this is the case, but other times it's not. The next time you come across the opportunity to stand up for someone, to compliment someone, to express yourself to someone, the next time you come across the opportunity to remind someone they are important, or to make someone smile, do not pass it up. You never know how much a missed opportunity may impact your life or the lives of others.

<u>18</u>

One of the things we often forget about others is that we are all on this *Pale Blue Dot* for the same reason, living. Life does not exist without relationships; humans are social creatures and one of the best and most rewarding things we can do during our time alive on Earth is to relate to others. When you get angry with someone . . . remind yourself they are human. When someone cuts us off in traffic . . . remind yourself they are human. When you judge someone, laugh at someone, hurt someone, when someone forgets your birthday . . . remind yourself they are human. We all have our stories, complete with joy, pain, love, and loss. We all have good days and bad days, and we all have moments when we feel invincible and when we feel worthless. The important thing to remember is that no matter how alone you may feel, no matter how isolated, someone, somewhere understands what you are going through, and you are never alone. Even though you may never meet that person, you may never know exactly what they are going through; we are all connected in more ways than one. There have only been roughly 100 billion people who have ever lived. That's it. Hundred billion, 7.6 billion of which are currently alive. That means that every single one of us is related. How would our outlook on life and others change if we assumed that we each had the same blood running through our veins? The same atoms and electrons? Nelson Mandela once said: "A fundamental concern for others in our individual and community lives would go a long way in making the world the better place we so passionately dreamt of." I think we could all do with this reminder occasionally.

<u>19</u>

Someone you know is being too hard on themselves. Someone you know feels like they're drowning. They feel like they can't keep up. They feel like no matter what they do they can't get a break. Maybe they haven't been as productive as they think they should be. Maybe they haven't exercised enough. Maybe they're not making enough money. Or perhaps they just feel they aren't where they're supposed to be in life. Our thoughts, words, and actions towards them can greatly impact this person and we may not even be aware of it. There's a phenomenon called the Pygmalion Effect. It's defined by a sequence of events whereby our thoughts about someone influence our actions towards them, which impacts their thoughts about themselves. This causes them to act in a way that further reinforces our beliefs about them, good or bad. Maybe someone is struggling but because they've always been the strong person, we treat them as such, which leads them to believe they need to drive on, to hide what they may be feeling, which only further reinforces your thoughts about them. Narratives feed our minds and these narratives guide what we do and do not do. These narratives have the power to propel and dispel, to push you forward, and to remove limitations, but they can also hold you back, dim your light. Make sure you tell this person that you're not expecting them to be perfect, that they can rest, that they have help, support, and love. Make sure you tell them that sometimes their best is just waking up, just being there. Make sure you let them know how appreciative you are of who they are and what they've done. Make sure you tell them they're loved. Even if that person is you . . . the only one in the room.

Epilogue

The phrase *The Only One in the Room* is not about standing out as much as it is about understanding the one thing you can control is yourself. Your thoughts, your words, and your actions are yours alone. Often, we feel obligated, we feel forced, we feel trapped, we feel helpless, but each day the sun will rise and set, and with the coming and going of the days you will always remain. *The Only One in the Room* speaks to understanding the difference between being *by* yourself and being *with* yourself. *The Only One in the Room* speaks to finding comfort in being with the person you truly are. No titles, no distractions, no masks.

If you have reached this point of this book my hope is that you have reflected and learned. I hope that you realize in one way or another, though you are the only one who can be you, you are not alone in your quest for life, joy, peace, and the never-ending pursuit of happiness. My goal in life is to let each person I interact with know they are loved, they are seen, and they are not alone, in the hopes that someone who feels like they have no one, or have no other choice, can see that outstretched hand and grasp onto someone who wants them to know how incredible they truly are.

Marlon M. Woods

The Only One in the Room

Printed in Great Britain
by Amazon